It's No Problem!

Nira Harel

It's No Problem!

Illustrated by Ora Eytan

Kestrel Books

To Assaf, who's already been stitched up twice!

Translated from the Hebrew
by Tamar Berkowitz

KESTREL BOOKS
Published by Penguin Books Ltd
Harmondsworth, Middlesex, England

Originally published in Israel by Massada Ltd, Publishers,
1980

First published in Great Britain, 1984

ISBN 0 7226 5952 0

Printed in Israel by Peli Printing Works Ltd

CONTENTS

WHAT'S MORE FRIGHTENING?

My name is Sam
and I live in a block of flats.
In the entrance hall
there's a switch for the
light on the stairs.
Everyone says that
it's no problem
to turn on the light
and go up the stairs.

But I'm scared to go up
the stairs on my own...
scared... scared...
It's dark there and
I can see spooky shadows
and I keep thinking
that someone
is hiding on the stairs,
waiting to attack me.

So I ask my mother
to come down and fetch me.
My friend Michael says,
'Why isn't
anyone else scared?
Why is it only you?'
But I just want
to be like everyone else!

I walked home from school
with Sharon and Toby.
Mum called out from the balcony,
'I'll be down in a minute to get you.'
Suddenly I heard myself saying,
'It's all right,
I'll come up on my own.'
Just like that,
the words popped out of my mouth!

I went into the entrance hall
and quickly turned on the light.
I ran up the two flights of stairs
and I met Michael,
so we went up
to my flat together to play.

Michael was scared
of my big spotty dog.
'Why aren't you afraid of him?'
he asked me.
'You just have to get
used to a dog,' I said,
'the dark
is much more frightening.'
Then we had some coke.

BIG BROTHER, LITTLE BROTHER

My big brother hit me again.
He's a horrible brother!
He's always bossing me about.
So what if he is bigger
and stronger than me?
Do I have to do
what he tells me to?
No, I DO NOT!

Dad says it was my fault
for starting the quarrel.
He says I tease my brother
and annoy him.
My parents always
get cross with me.
My brother gets away
with everything,
just because he's big.

My friend Michael
has a baby brother.
Lucky him,
that must be fun.
But I've just got
a big brother.

A boy in the playground
took my ball away
and wouldn't give it back.
I told him he was asking
for trouble but he laughed
and called me a baby.
So I called my big brother.
He came down and
grabbed the boy
who then started to cry
and gave me back my ball.
Cowardy custard!

That boy doesn't bother me any more,
he knows that my brother
can beat him up.
All the children round here know
that my big brother
is very strong.

Mum told me that we're going
to have a baby and that's great.
Because when I have a little brother
I can boss him about,
and take care of him.

THEY STITCHED ME UP

One afternoon we were playing
in the garden. We had a race to see
who could get to the door first.
I fell and crashed into the stairs
and hit my chin.
It hurt and I cried.
A lot of blood poured out
and it was a bit frightening.
Everyone shouted to my mother
to come downstairs because
I'd cut my chin. Mum cleaned
the cut and said we had
to go to the hospital.

She didn't tell me what they'd do to me
in the hospital and I was scared.
Perhaps they'd stitch me up?
How do you stitch up a chin?
With a needle and thread? Does it hurt?
I was so frightened
that I kept asking questions all the time.

At the hospital
we went into a huge room.
There were lots of ill people there,
lying in beds.
Some of them
were hidden behind curtains.

There were
some children there too.
One had a big cut
on his head
and another one
had been bitten by a dog.
You could tell
they were more seriously hurt
than I was
because you could see
lots more blood.

Then a doctor,
who was actually quite friendly,
explained that they had
to give me an injection.
I was really scared because
I'd never had an injection before.

The injection hurt
but I hardly felt the stitching at all.
They'll take out the stitches in a week's time.
That's a frightening thought too,
but not as frightening
as thinking about the stitching.

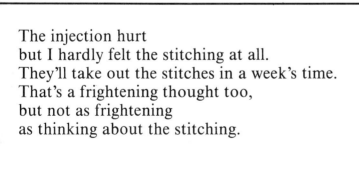

JUST AN HOUR LATE!

My name is Jill and Sam's my friend.
I went over to his home one afternoon
and he showed me the scar on his chin.
It's a nice pink scar and you can see
the holes the needle made.
Some time later
I looked out of the window
and saw that it was getting dark.

I ran home but when I got there
my parents shouted at me!
Mum shouted at me
then Dad shouted at me,
then they both shouted together.
I've never seen them so angry.
'What a thoughtless,
naughty girl!' they said.
'She goes out
and comes back late!
She can't be trusted.'
And this girl
they're talking about is — me!

My parents make a lot of fuss
about everything.
Nothing could have happened
to me, could it?
They're such old worriers!
So what if I was a bit late?
I was only about an hour late
after all!

Mum and Dad have gone out
to the cinema and haven't come back yet.
They always come back
at ten o'clock
but now it's eleven.

Perhaps something's happened to them
on the way?
Perhaps they've had an accident?
After all, it's difficult to see in the dark.
Why don't they come home?
Grown-ups are lucky,
they can go out at night whenever they want.
Children can't make any comments about it.
It makes me very cross!

Mum and Dad came back from the film
and saw that I was still awake.
'You are a little worrier!' they said.
'So what if we are a bit late?
We're only about an hour late after all!'

FIRST TIME AWAY

We've been to visit
Grandma and Grandpa.
There are always lots of nice things
to eat in their house.
'Here's your favourite supper,
Sam,' said Grandma.
It was delicious!

Mum and Dad said they
were tired and that we had to go home.
Why do I always have to leave
just when I'm in the middle
of a game with Grandpa
— and winning?
I wanted to stay and play
some more games
with Grandpa so I told Dad
to come and fetch me
next morning.

I'm sure I want to stay.
I've never actually stayed
the night away from home before but,
well, there's always a first time
and it will be nice and grown-up.
When I watch my parents leave in their car
I wish a bit
that I was with them,
but I don't say anything.
After all, I'm a big boy now,
not a baby who has to be
with his mother all the time!

Grandpa is starting to yawn.
We've finished all the games.
I've eaten all the sweets Grandma gave me too.
But I'm not a bit sleepy
and how can you go to bed if you're not sleepy?
I wonder what Mum and Dad are doing now?
I bet they're missing me.

Then Dad arrives,
bringing me my pyjamas and toothbrush.
Luckily he happens to ask
if I want to go home already.
Suddenly I really feel sleepy!

EVERYONE EXCEPT ME

Everyone's got a bicycle, except me.
Even Henry has a bicycle
and he's practically a baby.
But I haven't got one.
Why don't they buy me a bicycle?
If I had a bicycle I'd have lots of friends.
But I haven't got a bicycle
and I haven't even got one friend.

Well, I have got a football,
but that's no good when all
the other children have got bicycles.
Mum and Dad say I'm a nuisance
because I keep talking about bicycles
and practise pedalling on the sofa,
and they send me out to play.

I took my football
down to the playground.
Everyone said 'Great!'
And they wanted to play with it.
We threw it around
and played football for a long time.

Jim's got a red bicycle.
It's a bit small so
he has to stand up
on the pedals to ride it,
otherwise he bangs his knees
on the handlebars.
Jim thinks my football
is really good
and says
he wishes he had one too.

Mum promised that she'd try
to find a second-hand bicycle
for my birthday.

Now that I've thought about it
I'm not so sure I want a bicycle.
Perhaps a pen-knife would be more useful.
Everyone has a pen-knife, except me.

A BROKEN GLASS

Smash! I've dropped the glass
on the floor and it's broken.
Now there'll be a row.
If only I hadn't started
to do the washing-up.

Dad will say,
'You're always breaking things,
you naughty boy!'
But when Mum breaks something
he never says a word to her.
Sometimes he even laughs!

Mum will be cross with me
and she'll lock me in the bathroom
to punish me.
I'll hate that.
The floor tiles are cold to sit on
and I know for a fact
that two big spiders live down the pipe
of the wash-basin.

Mum and Dad come into the kitchen
and they see the broken glass on the floor.
Then they look at my hands
to make sure that I haven't cut myself.

Dad says: 'Oh dear,
so we're one glass less.
Never mind.
Just be a little more careful next time.
Perhaps you should just wash up the plastic dishes...'
Mum is sorry about the glass but she isn't cross.
She says 'You were just trying to help,
so how could I be cross with you?'

So I carefully sweep up
the broken bits of glass
and throw them away.
Just because I've broken
a glass this time
doesn't mean
that I shouldn't try to help,
does it!

GRANDMA'S IN HOSPITAL

My Grandma is in hospital.
She's got to have an operation.
I don't know what's the matter with her
but I'm worried.
My friend Sam told me that
once they took his grandmother
to the hospital
but they never said what happened to her.
Now Sam has two grandfathers
and only one grandmother.

Mum told me that Grandma
was once a little girl like me
and she had parents too.
But that was a long time ago.
and now Grandma
is an old woman.

When I grow up
I think I'll be like my mother
and when I grow even older
I'll probably be like Grandma.
I wonder what will happen to me
after that?

I went to visit Grandma
in the hospital and I took her
some flowers and a drawing
I'd done of our house.
Grandma was very pleased
and said that
she'd be going home next week.
Her grey hair looked nice
and soft and wavy
against the pillow.

Afterwards I went to see Grandpa.
We played a game
with some little boats in the sink
and then I helped him
to make the supper.

I think when I'm a grandparent
I'll play with my grandchildren too.
But I've got lots of time till then!

THE NEW BABY

Mum and Dad told me
that soon we'll have a baby.
They're pleased about it
but I'm not sure.
What do I want a baby for?
It might just be a lot of bother for me.
What's more there isn't enough room
for it in my bedroom.

I know that Mum will spend
all her time looking after the baby
and she won't take any notice of me.
When people come to visit our house
they'll bring presents for the baby.
People always spoil babies.
And I'll just be Sam,
the baby's brother.

This is my little sister!
She's so tiny she's like a doll.
She sleeps nearly all the time
and doesn't understand anything
you say to her.

I help Mum to look after her.
It isn't difficult at all.
After all,
I'm her big brother Sam.

Wow!
I got some presents
in honour of my new sister.
It's just like a birthday.
My sister laughs
when I say coo-coo to her.
I think she probably already realizes who I am!
And there does seem to be enough space
in my bedroom after all.

A GROWN-UP PARTY

Dad said, 'Jill, after work I'll take you to a
party for grown-ups.'
I was really excited.
I'm lucky to have such a nice Dad.

All day long I got ready for the party.
I polished my blue shoes and put on my best
dress
and I brushed my hair three times.

I kept thinking how wonderful
it was to be going
to a party with my father.
I told all my friends that I was going out
with my Dad
and I sang my favourite song over
and over again.

That evening Dad came home from
work very, very late.
We were both tired but went
to the party anyway.

When we arrived at the party there were
lots of people there
and there wasn't any room to sit down.
People kept pushing me and treading on
my blue polished shoes.

There was such a lot of noise
that I couldn't hear anything!
Dad seemed to know lots of people
and they all talked together
and I was bored.

When we got home Dad said,
'Never mind, tomorrow we'll have a
party just for us,
at home.
It'll be much more fun!'
I'm really looking forward to it!

A BOTTLE OF LEMON JUICE

Mum asked me to go to the shop
and buy a bottle of lemon juice.
I was worried and kept wondering
what I'd do if I went to the shop
and it was shut.

And if it was open
how would I find the lemon juice
among all the other bottles?
What if Mum hadn't given me
enough money?

And what would I do
if I fell over on the way home
and dropped the bottle?

Then I stopped wondering
and started to run down
to the shop.
The door was open
and I went in.

The shopkeeper showed me
the shelf full of bottles
and helped me to take down
the bottle of lemon juice.
I gave him the money
and he gave me back some change.

I walked back home with the lemon juice
and Mum made some lemonade from it.
It tasted horrible!

WHY AM I NEVER ILL?

My friend Jim is ill.
I think he's very lucky!
It means that he can stay at home
and watch television all day long.

Jim's mother
doesn't go out to work.
When Jim's at home
they can play games
and she reads stories
to him.

All the children in Jim's class at school
draw pictures for him
and take him presents.
When Jim comes back to school
the teacher is very nice to him
and asks him how he is.
Why am I never ill?

I've got a temperature
and I don't feel well.
My throat hurts a lot
and my head aches.
My eyes keep watering all the time
and I can't even watch television.

The doctor gave me some medicine
which tastes horrible.
Mum is busy
working in the kitchen all day
and I'm very bored.

Thank goodness I feel better today.
The schoolteacher brought along
some hamsters to show us today.
One hamster stuffed a whole handful
of sunflower seeds
in the pouches in his cheeks.

My friend Sally is away ill today.
I bet she's having a nice time!

A BAD MOOD

I had another argument
with Mum today.
We've had
a lot of arguments lately.
Nothing I do seems right.
Everything annoys her.
What can be the matter with her?

Mum hardly ever shouts
at my little sister.
You'd think Gloria was an angel
or something.
Anyway my mother thinks she is.

Perhaps Mum loves Gloria
and doesn't love me?
I keep thinking about this
and it makes me feel bad-tempered.

This evening
I saw that Mum's eyes were red.
She was trying not to show it
but I knew that she'd been crying.
I hadn't done anything wrong
so why was she upset?

Mum and I ate supper together,
just the two of us.
Mum explained that she was very tired
because Dad is so busy these days
that she has to do everything on her own.
What's more, things aren't going well at work
and she's worried about Grandpa who isn't
feeling well.

I told Mum that I'd try to help.
I hadn't realized that things were so difficult for
her.
Mum said that she felt much better already
and suddenly I didn't feel so bad-tempered
either.

OUR GANG

Harold's gang
was in our garden
and everyone was playing
with my bats
and an old ball
which we'd found.
The ball didn't bounce properly.
Of course I'm in the gang too.
Harold said so.

Harold is the leader.
He's the strongest
and biggest of us!
Everyone in the gang
does what Harold says
and I do too.

Joey's got a new bicycle.
Harold kept asking to have a go on it
and said that if Joey let him
then he could be in the gang.

The gang went to Joey's garden to play
and Harold told me
that I wasn't in the gang any more.

Everyone does what Harold says,
because he's so strong.
I do what Harold says, too.

I was in our garden
and there was nothing to do.
It's boring being alone in the garden.
William came down
with his brother's old skate-board
and we rolled it up and down.
Afterwards Guy arrived
and the three of us played together.

I told William and Guy
that it would be a good idea
to form a gang.
They didn't belong to a gang
either so they agreed.
It's more fun
when you've got a gang.

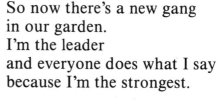

So now there's a new gang
in our garden.
I'm the leader
and everyone does what I say
because I'm the strongest.

Sally wants to join our gang
but we haven't decided yet
whether we'll accept her.
I need time to think about that.

THE BLOOD TEST

The doctor said
that I had to have a blood test.
I was worried about
how much blood they'd take out of me.
What if they took it all away
and I hadn't got any left?
Would my body fall down empty?

The grown-ups say
it won't really hurt
but then they would say
that wouldn't they!
Perhaps the pain will be awful
and I'll scream and
they'll just laugh
and say that I'm a baby!

Perhaps the nurse
who takes blood from children
is really a horrid witch?
Do I really have to have
this blood test?

We went to the hospital this morning
and waited for our turn.
There was another boy
of my age there.
We looked at each other for a while.
When I went into the laboratory
the nurse smiled at me.
She looked a bit like
Michael's mother
and was very friendly
and told me exactly
what she was going to do
and showed me her instruments.

Then the nurse put a needle in my finger
and suddenly
a big red drop of blood appeared.
I was rather surprised and said 'Ouch'.
It wasn't nice having a blood test
but it wasn't so terrible either.
There were lots of different bottles
in that room!

After a minute I went outside
holding a piece of cotton wool
on my finger.
Mum asked, 'Well?
What was it like?'
And we both laughed.
Then the other boy went in.

NO SCHOOL TODAY

When I arrived
at school this morning
I found that the door was locked.
Suddenly I remembered
that the whole school
had gone on a trip.
I'd forgotten all about it.
I'd missed the trip
and what's more
Mum and Dad were both at work
and there was no one at home.
I sat down on the step and cried.

Two of the mothers asked
if I wanted
to go home with them.
But I didn't want to.

A woman with a dog
asked me if I knew where my father worked.
Of course I knew!
I even knew the phone number.
The dog licked my hand.

We phoned my father
and he said
he'd come along right away
to fetch me.
The woman with the dog
waited with me.
She was so nice
and the dog wagged his tail!

Dad took me to his work with him
and gave me some paper to draw on.
Everyone in the office spoke to me.
Then Mum arrived
and we went to buy an ice-cream.
I'll have a lot to tell them
at school tomorrow!

A FRONT-DOOR KEY

I've got my own front-door key at last!
Everyone else in our family has a key.
So why shouldn't I have one too?
I'm big now!

Now I'll be able to get in
when there's no one at home
and I won't have to wait outside
on the steps.
It's so boring
being stuck outside
and waiting on the steps.

Michael has a door-key
and he goes into his flat
by himself every day
because his mother is out at work.
So I really wanted a key
of my own too!
And now I've got one!
From now on,
I can do whatever I want to
in the flat and no one can tell me off.
It's going to be fun.

So I ran home
to make sure that I was the first back.
I turned the key in the lock
and the door opened
and I walked in —
it wasn't difficult at all.

I drank some coke
and ate three sweets and chewed some gum
and ate a piece of chocolate cake
and a biscuit.
Then I looked out of the window.

Mum came back from work and asked
if I'd been all right on my own.
Then everyone asked me
if I'd been all right.
They kept asking
and it was nice telling them.
Tomorrow
I'll take the key to school with me
but I think I'll wait outside on the steps
until someone comes home.
It's no problem
being at home on one's own
but it's not much fun either!

A BORING HOLIDAY

What a boring holiday!
It goes on and on and there's nothing to look
forward to.
All the other children have gone out
and I haven't got anyone to play with.

My friends always have a nice time.
I'm the only one who doesn't go anywhere.
I'm just stuck here sitting in the garden.
For ever!

Our garden must be the most boring place in
the world.
There's nothing to do here.
Mum and Dad ought to take me out once,
anyway.

Mum and Dad took me to town.
We went to all the places grown-ups like to go
to, restaurants and shops.
It was very boring!
I didn't meet a single child I knew.

When we got home I went into the garden.
All the other children were there.
'Where were you today?' they asked.
'We had so much fun in the garden!'

I think they were probably just saying that
but I felt very cross anyway.
Just when something interesting happens
in the garden I have to go out.
This is really such a boring holiday!